TO:

_____

FROM:

_____

DATE:

_____

Still the

CELEBRATING THE MOTHER-DAUGHTER BOND

Person I Turn To

ANNA HELENE KIRSCH

SHAW

WATERBROOK
PRESS

Still the Person I Turn To: Celebrating the Mother-Daughter Bond
A SHAW BOOK
PUBLISHED BY WATERBROOK PRESS
2375 Telstar Dr., Suite 160
Colorado Springs, Colorado 80920
A division of Random House, Inc.

ISBN 0-87788-401-3

Copyright © 2001 by Lil Copan

Design by Uttley/DouPonce DesignWorks, Sisters, Oregon

Cameo photograph on page 79 used by permission of Maria Rooney.

For further acknowledgments please see page 112.

SHAW BOOKS and its circle of books logo are registered trademarks of WaterBrook Press, a division of Random House, Inc.

Library of Congress Cataloging-in-Publication Data
Copan, Lil.
  Still the Person I Turn To: Celebrating the mother-daughter bond/ by Anna Helene Kirsch
      p. cm.
ISBN 0-87788-401-3
1. Mothers and daughters—Miscellanea. 2. Mothers and daughters—Anecdotes. 3. Mothers and daughters—
Quotation, maxims, etc. I. Title.

HQ755.85.C666 2001
306.874'3—dc21   01-050225

Printed in the United States of America
2001—First Edition

10 9 8 7 6 5 4 3 2 1

To Mom

with loving thanks for giving your daughters the best place to start

And to Oma

CONTENTS

*W*hat is it that makes the mother-daughter relationship unlike any other? We share the language of the heart, a language *all* mothers and daughters instinctively understand. We find words that move us—to laughter, to tears, to affirmation. In these pages mothers and daughters speak these words to share their understanding of the wonder, the challenges, and the tenderness of this unique relationship.

But what moves us more than words is the reality of *love*. Love is the living, breathing picture of that commitment we have for each other. This through-it-all love carries us even when things are not smooth sailing, when tensions are high or misunderstandings arise. The very quality of love is its endurance, which makes love superior to any other thing. This is the meaning of the God-breathed words, "the greatest of these is love."

God has given us one of life's greatest gifts in this treasured kinship. We continually cherish it. Here, we celebrate it.

Making a decision to have a child

is momentous—it is to decide forever to have your heart

go walking around outside your body.

—Elizabeth Stone

MY LITTLE ONE

No one without experience knows
the anguish which children can cause and yet be loved.

—ELISABETH OF BRAUNSCHWEIG

We're taking a survey," she says, half joking. "Do you think I should have a baby?"

"It will change your life," I say carefully. I want her to know what she will never learn in childbirth classes: That the physical wounds of childbearing heal but that becoming a mother will leave an emotional wound so raw that she will be forever vulnerable.

I feel I should warn her that no matter how many years she has invested in her career, she will be professionally derailed by motherhood. She might arrange for childcare, but one day she will be going into an important business meeting, and she will think about her baby's sweet smell. She will have to use every ounce of discipline to keep from running home, just to make sure her child is all right.

However decisive she may be at the office, she will second-guess herself constantly as a mother. She will never feel the same about herself. That her life will be of less value to her once she has a child. That she would give it up in a moment to save her offspring, but will also begin to hope for more years—not to accomplish her own dreams, but to watch her children accomplish theirs.

—DALE HANSON BOURKE, *Everyday Miracles*, adapted

The highest

manifestation of love in the realm of the finite:

a mother's love for her child.

—EDITH DEEN

Family Living in the Bible, adapted

The birth of my own babies (every woman's Christmas) shows me that the power which staggers with its splendor is a power of love, particular love. Surely it takes no more creative concentration to make a galaxy than a baby. And surely the greatest strength of all is this loving willingness to be weak, to share, to give utterly.

— Madeleine L'Engle
WinterSong

Over the years I have learned that motherhood is much like an austere religious order, the joining of which obligates one to relinquish all claims to personal possessions.

— Nancy Stahl
If It's Raining, It Must Be the Weekend

Through wisdom a house is built,

And by understanding it is established;

By knowledge the rooms are filled

With all precious and pleasant riches.

—PROVERBS 24:3-4, NJKV

No question about it—motherhood does seem to be a thankless vortex some days. Yet I need to realize that mothers run in highly important circles. It's easier to understand that truth when I remember that God trusted His only Son to the care of a mother.

—SUSAN L. LENZKES
When the Handwriting on the Wall Is in Brown Crayon

She was born to me and she was born a girl. And I was born to my mother and I was born a girl. All of us are like stairs, one step after another, going up and down, but all going the same way.

—AMY TAN
The Joy Luck Club

Children use the

same part of my head as poetry does.

To deal with children is a matter of terrific imaginative identification.

And the children have to come first.

It's no use putting off their evening meal for two months.

—LIBBY HOUSTON

adapted

*M*iss Fairfax and her mother heard her scream and ran to the window. "Horrors!" said Miss Fairfax. "It's the bees! I told her not to . . ." But Joy's mother did not wait to hear what Miss Fairfax had told Joy. She ran into the garden, toward the terrified little girl with the great bee buzzing round her head. "Get behind me, Joy," she shouted. "Quick! Hide!"

Joy darted behind her mother, and the bee, alighting on the bare outstretched arm, gave her mother a good sting. It then flew over her shoulder and continued to buzz round Joy.

"He's after me!" screamed Joy.

"No, he's not," said her mother. "It's all over. Stop being frightened. Look at my arm—there's his sting. Bees only sting once. You're quite safe now."

Joy stared at the big red welt that was beginning to rise on her mother's arm. She was shaking and very near to tears.

Joy was very quiet while she ate her tea and sat as close to her mother as she could. She kept glancing at the red swelling on her mother's arm, but she did not say anything about it till bedtime, when her mother came to say good night.

"I'm sorry, Mummy," whispered Joy from somewhere down under the bedclothes. "I'll never do something like that again. It was me that ought really to have got stung, wasn't it?"

"Very true," her mother replied. "But all the same, I'm glad it was me."

"Why?" said Joy, appearing suddenly over the top of the sheet.

"Because I love you. Now, go to sleep."

— PATRICIA ST. JOHN
Stories to Share

Mother guilt. It comes with the birth,

is brought forth from us with the placenta, grows like the piles of laundry,

and stays with us forever, like we believe the child will.

— ABIGAIL STONE

"Bye Bye Baby"

Adorable children are considered

to be the general property of the human race.

(Rude children belong to their mothers.)

— JUDITH MARTIN

Miss Manners' Guide to Rearing Perfect Children

*A*t that time in my life my mother was always right. If, for example, she said, "Take your umbrella. It's going to rain," I took it and it did. If she said, "You may wear a sweater today instead of your coat," she was right. The air was warm. Once I thought I knew better than she did when she said, "Take your mittens. It's going to snow." I didn't, and it did.

So naturally I became a docile and obedient daughter. After all, what was the use of deliberately courting disaster?

—Caryl Porter

Harvest from a Small Vineyard

Obey God, the emperor, and your mother.

— ELISABETH OF BRAUNSCHWEIG

"Mother, may I go out to swim?"

"Yes, my darling daughter.

Hang your clothes on a hickory limb,

And don't go near the water."

— AMERICAN RHYME

A sick child is always the mother's property,

her own feelings generally make it so.

—JANE AUSTEN

Persuasion

In the eyes of its mother every beetle is a gazelle.

—AFRICAN PROVERB

All the earth, though it were full of kind hearts, is but a desolation and a desert place to a mother when her only child is absent.

—ELIZABETH GASKELL
My Lady Ludlow

Raising a child is like building a kite. You must bend the twigs enough, but not too much, for you might break them. You must find paper that is delicate and light enough to wave on the breath of the wind, yet must withstand the ravages of a storm. You must tie the strings gently but firmly so that it may not fall apart. You must let the string go, eventually, so that the kite will stretch its ambition. It is such delicate work, Lord, being a mother.

—HELENA MARIA VIRAMONTES

Sleep, my little one, sleep,

Your father is tending the sheep.

Your mother shakes the little tree . . .

Down tumbles a lovely dream,

Sleep, my little one, sleep.

— GERMAN LULLABY

The "setting free" of my daughter was the
most difficult part in our relationship. There is a natural desire
to clutch and cling; it takes all one's self-discipline to say "good-bye"
without whining or holding anything back.
Now is when one prays that the foundation that was laid
holds firm. We transform our tendency to worry into the weapon
of prayer—the ultimate tool of a mother.

—ELFI GEBHART

LINES OF BEAUTY

Listening to a speaker describe the finishing touches on an eagle's nest,

I was pierced by the mother eagle's investment in her home.

It seems that once she builds the eight-foot by ten-foot monstrous nest,

she then softens the nest by plucking down from her own chest.

Adding a fluffy bit here and there,

like pillows accenting a color scheme in a living room,

the mother eagle completes her nest with an offering of her own body.

—ELISA MORGAN

Meditations for Mothers, adapted

My Daughter

I watch you from the window with your friends rocking the trailer, *bump* to one end, *bump* to the other, a gaggle of twelve-year-olds laughing down the petals from the plum tree, waiting for my voice to scold, to stop your fun and mouth the usual *this will wreck your father's trailer—I've told you enough times before.* But my expected words will have to wait, for I am watching how my daughter laughs, her head tossed back, her hair splayed out like wings, her mouth a nearly perfect "O." She grabs the elbow of her friend to keep from falling, dizzy from the spell of laughter, the world a blur of new spring leaves and sidewalks. She is beautiful, I think, a little ashamed of myself for such vanity, for an indulgence scorned by my mother and her mother before her.

I cannot disappoint them any longer. Opening the front door is enough to make the rocking stop, the laughter turn to giggles. I say my piece and watch my daughter's face—controlled, accepting, almost a woman's now, as she watches me turn before the door closes softly behind me.

—Miriam Pederson

And for the three magic gifts

I needed to escape the poverty of my hometown,

I thank my mother,

who gave me a sewing machine, a typewriter, and a suitcase.

— ALICE WALKER

In Search of Our Mothers' Gardens

The first time I left home for boarding school, I laid in bed that night and felt the whole world crush me because I was growing up, leaving home, slipping away from who I was into a world of who I would become. The night lasted so long. And I wanted to call my mom the next morning to make sure she was there, at the other end of the line, the other end of the country, the other end of the world. But I couldn't call, and my fears just floated in the air, like the heavy wet laundry my mom would hang out in the basement. Just there. Sad. And this was life. The saddest things were the beginnings of growing up.

—EDDMA BURMAE

Amy Tan, author of *The Joy Luck Club,* says she didn't think she'd ever be able to fulfill her parents' expectations:

If I got straight A's, they'd want straight A-pluses. If I got straight A-pluses, I'd have to win a Rhodes scholarship. When I finished *The Joy Luck Club,* it went on the *New York Times* bestseller list at No. 4, way beyond anyone's expectations. My mother said, "Hmmm. No. 4. Who is this No. 3? No. 2? No. 1?" But right after that, she said, "I'm not disappointed you're No. 4; I just think you're so good that you deserve to be No. 1." It finally hit me. I remember being so angry when I was younger, not understanding.

I brought her to a talk I gave, and she sat stone-faced throughout the whole reading, never changing her expression. "Did you like what I read?" I asked her when it was over.

"I wasn't listening," she replied. "All I could do was look at you and say, 'That's my daughter.'"

We want more from our

mothers than they are ever able to give us,

and becoming aware of this pitfall should help us manage

the relationships we have with our own daughters.

—ELAINE MCEWAN
My Mother, My Daughter

We learn how to be women from our mothers.

They teach us, consciously and unconsciously, what women are.

—JUDITH ARCANA
Our Mothers' Daughters

When daughters are on the way from home,

be it for the afternoon or a lifetime,

a loving mother will disguise her agony with trifles.

—KAYE GIBBONS

On the Occasion of My Last Afternoon

That our daughters may be as corner stones,

polished after the similitude of a palace.

—PSALM 144:12, KJV

How to match the girls

we were to the women we became?

—BONNIE FRIEDMAN

Images

My daughter has her braces removed and contemplates entering high school. In the morning, we share the bathroom mirror — her preoccupation measured against mine in the silvery likeness — her eyes bright and anxious, mine strained, baffled at the way time distances the body from the self. We are sisters for a moment — grinning at this occasion when we, thirty-six years apart, preen and raise our eyebrows in the joy of femininity. Then the words, "You'd better hurry. It's getting late . . ." defines the space between us, the '50s, '60s, '70s and '80s displaying themselves like fashion models, shedding the poodle skirt, the tent dress, the mini-skirt and midi at terrible speed.

What can I wish for this replica of myself, caught in the cusp of the twenty-first century? What is the remedy for heartsickness, homesickness, restless yearning that will fill her days, that will ask her to succumb or flee? How can she finally know who she is through the eyes of God who knows her, made her in His image, is perfecting her?

— Miriam Pederson

41

Love never gives up.

Love cares more for others than for self.

Love doesn't want what it doesn't have.

Love doesn't strut,

Doesn't have a swelled head,

Doesn't force itself on others,

Isn't always "me first,"

Doesn't fly off the handle,

Doesn't keep score of the sins of others,

Doesn't revel when others grovel,

Takes pleasure in the flowering of truth,

Puts up with anything,

Trusts God always,

Always looks for the best.

—1 CORINTHIANS 13:4-7, THE MESSAGE

The relationship between adult women
and their own mothers is perhaps the most complex
and emotionally charged of all relationships
within the family.

—B. J. COHLER AND H. U. GRUNEBAUM

A Particular Friendship

What's more, Mama, other than you,
there are very few people who will understand
what it is that I am saying.

—SDIANE BOGUS
"Mom de Plume" in *Double Stitch*

I am forty-one years old, and my mother is seventy-six.
She is still the person I turn to. You feel you're
imposing when you ask friends to help. But
you don't feel that way if you ask your mother.

—KATHY ALCORN
"This Time with My Mother Has Been
Like a Gift" in *Mothers Talking*

I was married for three years before I had my girl, Jane. You don't know how many times I'd wish and wish and wish. God heard my prayers. Childbirth didn't mean anything to me because I had to wait a long time for her. I wouldn't have complained anyhow because she's a wonderful gal, even today. She's sixty-one now. We're pals just like my mother was with me, two good pals.

—JANE HOPPER
"I'm on My Soapbox"

She discovered with great delight
that one does not love one's children
just because they are one's children
but because of the friendship formed
while raising them.

—GABRIEL GARCÍA MÁRQUEZ

49

The relationship between

mothers and daughters is so much more complex than

even the relationship between a man and a woman.

It's so primal, you can never escape it.

—NAOMI JUDD

No matter how old a mother is,

she watches her middle-aged children for signs of improvement.

—FLORIDA SCOTT-MAXWELL

The Measure of My Days

But most of all

is the way you loved me,

loved me like I want to love

and rarely can.

—ELLEN BASS
from "For My Mother"

My apartment is the home of someone who is not a homemaker, someone who listens to the messages on the answering machine and then runs out again.

But she would not criticize me as other mothers might. Instead she would buy me things, a cheap but pretty print she would mat herself, a throw of some kind. And as she arranged the throw or hung the picture, she would say, smiling, "We're so different, aren't we, Ellie?"

But she would never realize as she said it, as she'd said it so many times before, that if you are different from a person everyone agrees is wonderful, it means you are somehow wrong.

— ANNA QUINDLEN

One True Thing

My mother phones daily to ask,

"Did you just try to reach me?"

When I reply, "No," she adds, "So, if you're not too busy,

call me while I'm still alive,"

and hangs up.

—ERMA BOMBECK

Since I saw her last she has entered into old age.
The masks have been thrust off and she has regained
the ability to pass rapidly from one pure state of
feeling to another. Above all, she loves with such
intensity that she cannot keep still. And so she cries
out, "What shall I do with all this joy? Do you
know how happy you have made me? How will I
keep it inside?" And then she presses her hand to
her heart and squeezes down, her eyes spilling.

—KIM CHERNIN
In My Mother's House

How shall I write of my mother?

She is so near to me that it almost seems

indelicate to speak of her.

—HELEN KELLER

The Story of My Life

A mother understands what a child does not say.

—HEBREW PROVERB

Shortly after my mother died there were many things I missed about her—but there was a curious thing I realized I missed, which I never expected—I missed knowing that there was someone out there who "worried" about me. My mother was concerned about every area of my life (big and small), and now there is no one out there who is quite so concerned. And in every area I knew she only wished me the best.

— MARTHA M. KOHL

ou have to do this," she added, rubbing my fingers as though I was a child who

had come in from the cold. "You would want your daughter to do it for you."

"Jules, what about my life?"

"What about it? It's not forever. . . . But the truth is that she's your mother, and she needs you

for a while, and you get your life back at the end and you've done the right thing."

— ANNA QUINDLEN

One True Thing

Most of all,

love each other as if your life depended on it.

Love makes up for practically anything.

—1 PETER 4:8, THE MESSAGE

Nothing can fill the gap when we are away from those we love, and it would be wrong to try and find anything. We must simply hold out and win through. That sounds very hard at first, but at the same time it is a great consolation, since leaving the gap unfilled preserves the bond between us. It is nonsense to say that God fills the gap; he does not fill it, but keeps it empty so that our communion with one another may be kept alive, even at the cost of pain.

—Dietrich Bonhoeffer

You ask me about my future,
and I tell you about my children.

—SUSAN GRIFFIN

HEIRLOOMS

Girl, we come from a long line
of strong and going on women;
we don't let nothing keep us down.

—AFRICAN-AMERICAN SAYING

Today I watch my daughter go bounding, tireless, down the hill of our backyard to the town forest (she so loves the woods), and I wonder if she will be a dancer or a painter or a writer or a teacher or a social reformer—or maybe a forest ranger. It is May, and here in New England little splashes of lavender and purple and white are just beginning to appear among grass that is trying to return to green.

I scoop my daughter in my arms, wriggling (she wants to stay outside), and in the kitchen pour her apple juice in a tippy cup and myself hot tea in a cup left me by my grandmother. And my daughter and I drink to the intricate, mysterious chain of life.

—JOY JORDAN-LAKE
Grit and Grace, adapted

In the end did I find the secret, and it was this: There is no one secret way to be a "good" mother. Each of us has to invent motherhood for herself and invent it over and over and over as we move forward through it. We can find the common threads of motherhood from talking to each other, but everyone is different. Each child is different, and we are different with each child, just as life is different for each child. No one explains how to do it. Each of us must figure it out for ourselves.

—FRANCES WELLS BURCK

Mothers Talking

69

The most remarkable thing

about my mother is that for thirty years she served

the family nothing but leftovers.

The original meal has never been found.

— CALVIN TRILLIN

Recently, my mother was asked what had been her secret to peace. . . . Her reply was simple. As she picked up an old childhood Bible she had found tucked away, she said, "I was able because of the written and living Word of God." From our earliest days, she instilled in us that same love and dependency on the person of Jesus Christ and in His written Word, the Bible.

—GIGI GRAHAM TCHIVIDJIAN
A Search for Serenity

Although my mother has been gone

for almost forty years, even after all these decades

she is still my ideal for my walk with God.

—KATHARINA NEUBACHER

Her children rise up and call her blessed.

— PROVERBS 31:28, NKJV

Our mother-daughter
relationships are worthy of all the
time and effort that we can
devote to them.
We will deeply regret doing
anything less.

—ELAINE MCEWAN
My Mother, My Daughter

My mother once framed a snapshot taken on an early spring visit to my grandmother in Birmingham, Alabama, in which I, a child of three, had picked violets from the side of the road and was presenting my beloved grandmother's favorite flower to her proudly, ceremoniously, as Gawain might have produced the Grail. The picture was shot beneath the oak tree that stood in what once was my great-grandmother's front yard. Three heads of curly hair blowing in the spring breeze are there beneath the ancient tree: my mother is the smiling spectator, as my grandmother bends over me in an almost greedy solicitude. Four generations, if you count the oak.

I always loved that photograph taken on my great-grandmother's front yard. It said something powerful to me as a child about what it was to be female—and in particular, what it was to be female in my family. Violets and oaks, I understood that picture to explain, are what you come from. Violets and oaks have given something of their lives to give you strength as well as grace.

—JOY JORDAN-LAKE, *Grit and Grace*

And in this rather complicated

household my mother brought us up to love God and

to love all things beautiful and to laugh.

—PATRICIA ST. JOHN

An Ordinary Woman's Extraordinary Faith

We share one another's past as no one else
can. The ties that inextricably bind our
hearts include the shared memories of our
common history. One word is often
enough to awaken memories long
dormant. A meaningful glance confirms
the recollection and strengthens and
deepens the rich tie we call family.

—HELEN COPAN NEUBACHER

The thoughts of a daughter are a kind of memorial.

—ENID BAGNOLD

The Chalk Garden

A COLLECTION OF MEMORIES

You never get over being a child,

as long as you have a mother to go to.

—SARAH ORNE JEWETT

The Country of Pointed Firs

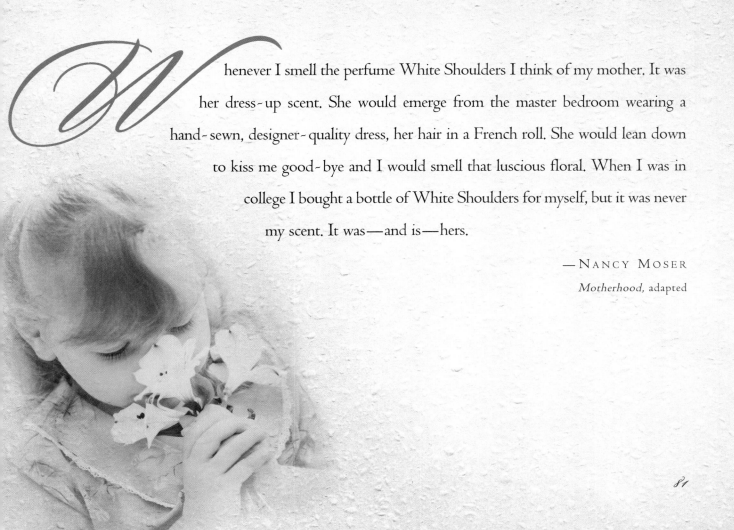

*W*henever I smell the perfume White Shoulders I think of my mother. It was her dress-up scent. She would emerge from the master bedroom wearing a hand-sewn, designer-quality dress, her hair in a French roll. She would lean down to kiss me good-bye and I would smell that luscious floral. When I was in college I bought a bottle of White Shoulders for myself, but it was never my scent. It was—and is—hers.

—NANCY MOSER
Motherhood, adapted

Yours the voice

Sounding ever in my ears.

—MADELEINE MASON-MANHEIM
from "To My Mother" in *Hill Fragments*

I feel shelter to speak to you.

—EMILY DICKINSON

By and large, mothers and
housewives are the only workers
who do not have regular time off.
They are the great vacationless class.

—ANNE MORROW LINDBERGH

Now we pull the corners taut and slip them under the
mattress. My mother passes her hand over the blanket and
I recall how much I loved this gesture when I was a girl,
believing it made sleep possible and kept it peaceful.

—KIM CHERNIN

In My Mother's House

"Let's go to your room. I'll lie down with you," her mother said.

"It won't help."

But it did.

—ANNE LAMOTT

Crooked Little Heart

Most mothers are instinctive philosophers.

—HARRIET BEECHER STOWE
The Minister's Wooing

One mother achieves more than a hundred teachers.

—HEBREW PROVERB

Sorely troubled, Mother watched me and groped for words that might help. Yet she knew her words would make little difference at the moment. It was enough that she was there to listen. . . . She understood my need for an answer to my agonizing question. . . . Where is the God of love who cares about the individual in what has happened? . . . She knew that my great need was still to be oriented to God, centered in Him, so that my life would have an anchor. But she also knew that this could not be forced. "In God's own time," she told me quietly, "you will get God's answers."

— CATHERINE MARSHALL
To Live Again

I, like many women, seem to have amassed this storehouse of motherly nuggets I draw on periodically with my own daughter. Some I heard from my own mother, some from other people's moms, and some I think I made up—either that, or they come encoded in the female chromosome. For example:

- Don't worry, you're just a late bloomer.
- They tease you because they like you.
- I don't mind the heal of bread (or the burned bacon, or the bitten-into piece of chocolate that nobody else wants because it's a funny orange flavor)
- What do you say?
- Never, never run holding a pencil. (Variations: scissors, lollipop in mouth.)

- There's nothing dirtier than money.

- Do you have everything?

- If your shoes look good, you look good.

- (On school mornings:) Let's just take your temperature and see how sick you really are.

- Let's see a smile on that pretty face.

- Don't worry about me. I'll be fine.

- Yes, I'm here.

—Elizabeth Cody Newenhuyse
Mothers and Daughters Together

My mother had never been content just to live and be comfortable. She always wanted something more—some form of beauty. She and I started going to art exhibits together when I was in the second grade. My mother loved the Impressionists, who blinded you with their light. I was sure they had been nearsighted to see the world in huge blurs of bright colors. One day when I was in the third grade, we saw a Rembrandt show in the morning and a Pierre Bonnard show after lunch. I didn't understand what longing for love or beauty had motivated her to take a nine-year-old daughter to two art exhibits in one day.

—KYOKO MORI
The Dream of Water

91

I cannot forget my mother.

Though not as sturdy as others, she is my bridge.

When I needed to get across,

she steadied herself long enough for

me to run across safely.

— RENITA WEEMS

"Hush, Mama's Gotta Go Bye-Bye"

My first vivid memory of you

Mamacita,

we made tortillas together—

yours perfect and round,

mine irregular and fat—

we laughed.

—ALMA LUZ VILLANUEVA
from "To Jesus Villanueva, With Love"

TO A MOTHER

Know, I am never far from you,

I bear you inwardly as you bore me—as intimately too

and as my flesh is of your own and our early mesh,

woven one so you are still my own

and everything about you, home,

the features, eyes, the hands,

your entire form are the past, present and to come,

the familiarity, the ease of my living, and my peace.

—SISTER MARY AGNES
Order of the Poor Clares

As we grow in the
experience of mothering our daughters,
we increasingly learn that prayer
accomplishes the things we
cannot carry out in ourselves—or in others.

—Debra Evans

Kindred Hearts

A Prayer for You

As a mother comforts her child,

so will I comfort you.

—ISAIAH 66:13, NIV

f I don't seem to need help, it is because I have a better friend, even than Father, to comfort and sustain me. My child, the trouble and temptations of your life are beginning , and may be many. Go to God with all your little cares, and hopes, and sins, and sorrows, as freely and confidingly as you come to your mother."

Jo's only answer was to hold her mother close, and, in the silence which followed, the sincerest prayer she had ever prayed left her heart without words. Led by her mother's hand, she had drawn nearer to the Friend who welcomes every child with a love stronger than that of any father, tenderer than that of any mother.

—LOUISA MAY ALCOTT

Little Women

I f only God would lean out of heaven and tell me that my children are going to make it, I could relax. But God doesn't do that. He tells us to be the parents he has called us to be in his strength and promises to do his part. Driven to prayer (after discovering that manipulation didn't work), I began to realize I was only truly positive and confident when I'd been flat on my face before the Lord.

—JILL BRISCOE
Marriage Matters! adapted

Lord,

you have been our dwelling place

throughout all generations.

—PSALM 90:1, NIV

Jesus, Son of human mother,

Bless our motherhood, we pray;

Give us grace to lead our children,

Draw them to thee day by day;

May our sons and daughters be

Dedicated, Lord, to thee.

— EMILY L. SHIRREFF
from "Gracious Savior, Who Didst Honor"

The day before Elisabeth Elliot was to sail to Ecuador to begin mission work her mother wrote:

My own dear Bets:

How inarticulate I feel at this moment, as I try to put into words my thankfulness to our Father for His good hand upon you over the years, for His faithfulness when I have been so faithless, for His calling you into His service and giving you grace and faith to be obedient, for giving you courage when the way seemed hard, and utter and complete trust each step of the way. You have been such a comfort and very real help to me spiritually. I will miss being able to pour out my "woes" to you, dear, but how I do thank God for you and that He is leading you. . . .

"Your life is hid with Christ in God"—the only safe place! God keep you, dear.

Loving you always,

Mother

—ELISABETH ELLIOT
The Shaping of a Christian Family

Every time you cross my mind,

I break out in exclamations

of thanks to God.

Each exclamation is a trigger to prayer.

I find myself praying for you

with a glad heart.

—PHILIPPIANS 1:3‒4, THE MESSAGE

*D*ear Loving God, thank you for creating my daughter's inmost being; for knitting her together in my womb. I praise you because she is fearfully and wonderfully made; your works are wonderful, I know that full well. Her frame was not hidden from you when she was made in the secret place. When she was woven together in the depths of the earth, your eyes saw her unformed body. All the days ordained for her were written in your book before one of them came to be. And today, God, these truths quiet me and give me great hope for her. Thank you.

—RUTH TUTTLE CONARD

Devotions for New Moms, based on Psalm 139:13-16

AS ANY MOTHER TO THE SAVIOR

As Thou didst walk the lanes of Galilee,

So, loving Savior, walk with her for me,

For since the years have passed and she is grown,

I cannot follow; she must walk alone.

Be Thou my feet that I have had to stay,

For Thou canst comrade her on every way;

Be Thou my voice when sinful things allure,

Pleading with her to choose those which endure.

Be Thou my hands that would keep hers in mine,

And all things else that mothers must resign.

When she was little, I could walk and guide,

But now I pray that Thou be at her side.

And as Thy blessed mother folded Thee,

So, loving Savior, fold my girl for me.

— UNKNOWN

But I have stilled and quieted my soul;

like a weaned child with its mother,

like a weaned child is my soul within me.

—PSALM 131:2, NIV

Let my children be committed to thy mercy.

—KATHERINE VON BORA

ABOUT THE COMPILER

ANNA HELENE KIRSCH is a penname to signify the composite of three daughters, Lil Copan, Helen Copan Neubacher, and Evelyn Copan Bute. In *Still the Person I Turn To,* they celebrate their mother, Valtraut Copan, and their mother's mother, Anna Helene Kirsch. A mother of seven and a grandmother of sixteen, Valtraut Copan (born in Riga, Latvia) lives a faithful and courageous life worthy of gratitude and honor. Here, her daughters commemorate the bond that has endured through generations of mothers and daughters.

Special thanks to the Copan family for the use of

photographs on pages 49, 53, 85, 87, 92, 106, and 108—with particular appreciation

for the pictures of Anna Helene Kirsch on pages 47 (left) and 63 (center).

Share Your Heart
with the Person
You Turn To

God has given you one of life's greatest gifts in the mother-daughter bond. Your treasured relationship is unlike any other, one you continually cherish, even when you are separated by long miles. You can celebrate it with the gift of a card at anytime and from any place.

DaySpring cards capture the language that brings hearts together, a language that mothers and daughters instinctively understand. Fresh art and the powerful connection of loving words and Scripture make the difference.

What better way to express your love than with a card?

You can find DaySpring cards at your favorite Christian bookstore.

ACKNOWLEDGMENTS

Excerpts taken from *Marriage Matters!* © 1994 by Jill and Stuart Briscoe; *Devotions for New Moms,* © 1996 by Ruth Conard; *Grit and Grace: Portraits of a Woman's Life,* © 1997 by Joy Jordan-Lake; *WinterSong,* © 1997 by Madeleine L'Engle and Luci Shaw; *Motherhood,* © 1997 by Nancy Moser; *Mothers and Daughters Together,* © 1999 by Harold Shaw Publishers; *An Ordinary Woman's Extraordinary Faith,* © 1996 by Patricia St. John; and *Stories to Share,* © 1997 by Patricia St. John are used by permission of Harold Shaw Publishers.

"Images" and "My Daughter," © 2001 by Miriam Pederson, are used by kind permission of the author.

Scripture quotations marked KJV are taken from the *King James Version* of the Holy Bible.

Scripture quotations marked NKJV are taken from the *New King James Version.* Copyright © 1982 by Thomas Nelson, Inc. Used by permission. All rights reserved.

Scripture quotations marked NIV are taken from the *Holy Bible, New International Version*®. NIV®. Copyright © 1973, 1978, 1984 by International Bible Society. Used by permission of Zondervan Publishing House. All rights reserved.

Scripture quotations marked THE MESSAGE are from *The Message.* Copyright © by Eugene H. Peterson 1993, 1994, 1995. Used by permission of NavPress Publishing Group.

Reasonable care has been taken to trace original ownership and, when necessary, obtain permission to reprint material in this book. For material not in the public domain, selections were made according to generally accepted fair-use standards and practices. Should any attribution be found to be incorrect, the publisher welcomes written documentation supporting correction for subsequent printings.